Prayers of Intercession

Book 1

Susan Sayers

First published in 1997 by
KEVIN MAYHEW LTD
Rattlesden
Bury St Edmunds
Suffolk IP30 0SZ

The prayers in this book were first published in *Intercessions
for the Church Year* (Kevin Mayhew, 1989, 1991, 1995) and
New Intercessions for the Church Year (Kevin Mayhew, 1995)

ISBN 0 86209 964 1
Catalogue No 1500093

0 1 2 3 4 5 6 7 8 9

Front cover: *White Lily Pads at Giverny*
by Agostini, Max or Max-Agostini (1914-97). Galerie Martin-Caille
Matignon, Paris/Bridgeman Art Library, London.

Cover design by Jaquetta Sergeant
Edited by Peter Dainty
Typesetting by Louise Hill
Printed and bound in Finland

Contents

Foreword

A long with Paul's famous trilogy of faith, hope and love, prayer is one of those vital threads which keeps the world in touch with the loving and sustaining power of God. Prayer sometimes seems so weak and ineffective compared with direct human action, but that is because we forget that it is a channel of the Spirit of God. Through prayer, the Spirit is able to flow into both Church and world to heal, renew, guide, strengthen and encourage all those caught up in the challenge and struggle of life.

These intercessions are intended for use wherever Christians meet to hold before God the needs and concerns of humankind, and to dedicate themselves to God's service. Each set of prayers deals with 'the Church', 'the world', 'the national and local community' and 'people in need', but covers different aspects of these subject areas each time. The comprehensive index will help users to find specific topics suitable for their needs. In the contents list the prayers are arranged in a more general way, based on the wording of the responses or a repeated phrase in the prayer itself. This will be helpful when choosing a set of intercessions to fit in with the theme of a service or sermon. The suggested responses are optional and though they offer the congregation an active role in the prayers, they may be adapted.

One of the most important features of these intercessions is the opportunity for silence (or for prayer contributions from members of the group). This serves two purposes. Firstly, it allows the prayers to be focused on named individuals and precise situations; and secondly, it gives room for listening to God as well as speaking to him. This will make those who pray more open to God's Spirit and more responsive to his direction, and, if so, one of the main purposes of prayer will surely have been fulfilled.

THE PUBLISHER

THE GREATNESS
OF GOD

You are our God

Father, let your Church be freshly inspired
to spread the gospel and serve the world
without thought of personal safety or comfort.
Silence for prayer
At all times and in all places
you are our God.

Father, raise up leaders in each community
who are honest and trustworthy,
and rekindle our enthusiasm
for honour and mutual respect.
Silence for prayer
At all times and in all places
you are our God.

Father, breathe into all our relationships
patience, understanding and affection,
keep marriages strong and friendships open-hearted.
Silence for prayer
At all times and in all places
you are our God.

Father, ease into wholeness the sick and the confused,
calm the fearful, soothe the sobbing,
unfasten the chained and let your love pour in.
Silence for prayer
At all times and in all places
you are our God.

Father, receive into your presence
the travellers who have come home to you,
and out of all evil and suffering bring good.

Silence for prayer

At all times and in all places
you are our God.

Father, may our praises and joyful thanks
be a sweet, fragrant offering at every part of our lives.

Silence for prayer

Father, your greatness
is beyond our understanding,
but knowing your love
we bring to you these prayers,
in the name of Jesus Christ, our Lord.
Amen.

The Lord our maker

Knowing that when we pray in faith
our loving Father will hear us,
let us pray together for the Church,
and for the world he has made.

Bless the work of all who spread
the wonderful news of your love.
May all who profess to be Christians
shine with your light so that others are drawn
to know your glory and experience
the joy of your peace.
Silence for prayer

Lord our maker,
hear our prayer.

Sustain and protect Elizabeth our Queen
and guide all world leaders, advisers and politicians
to act with wisdom and integrity.
Silence for prayer

Lord our maker,
hear our prayer.

Father, we commend to your loving keeping
all who have died, especially . . .
that they may live for ever
in the glorious peace and joy of your heaven.
Silence for prayer

Lord our maker,
hear our prayer.

We offer you thanks and praise
for the rich and beautiful world
you have provided for us,
and for the many blessings in our lives,
and for the gift of life itself.

Silence for prayer

Lord our maker,
hear our prayer.

Now let us bring
our personal requests to God
in quietness and trust.

Silence for prayer

Lord our maker,
**hear our prayer
which we offer in the name
of Jesus Christ, your Son.
Amen.**

The earth is the Lord's

Lord of the earth we stand on,
the air we breathe, the food we grow,
keep us in touch with this planet we inhabit;
help us to tend it well and enjoy its beauty.

Silence for prayer

Lord of heaven and earth,
let your kingdom come.

Lord of our past and our future,
Lord of our longings and disappointments,
teach us to recognise you in every moment
and know you are there
through the good and the bad times.

Silence for prayer

Lord of heaven and earth,
let your kingdom come.

Lord of our fears and uncertainties,
of our laughter and our foolishness,
fill us with thankfulness
and remind us of how great it is
to be alive.

Silence for prayer

Lord of heaven and earth,
let your kingdom come.

Lord of our families and our friends,
of those we like and those we don't;
breathe into our loving
the loving you show to us.

Silence for prayer

Lord of heaven and earth,
let your kingdom come.

Loving Father,
hear the prayers we offer,
and use our bodies, minds and spirits
in establishing your kingdom,
through Jesus Christ, our Lord.
Amen.

The goodness of God

Father, we remember our brothers and sisters in Christ
as they worship in large and small groups
all over the world.
Silence for prayer
O give thanks to the Lord
for he is good.

Father, we think of the world's peacemakers
and all who spend their lives
working constructively for good;
all who uphold Christian values and stand firm
for what is right.
Silence for prayer
O give thanks to the Lord
for he is good.

Father, we remember all who are
bringing their children up carefully and lovingly;
all who care for elderly neighbours and relatives;
all who work to build community where they live.
Silence for prayer
O give thanks to the Lord
for he is good.

Father, we think of the sick and those caring for them;
we think of those who rarely get a break,
but need one;
those who are offering their suffering for you to use.
Silence for prayer

O give thanks to the Lord
for he is good.

Father, we remember those who are dying
and those who have crossed from time into eternity;
we think of the example of their lives
and we remember those who love them.
Silence for prayer
O give thanks to the Lord
for he is good.

Father, we think of the beauty of all you have made
and the daily miracles of life and love.
Silence for prayer
O give thanks to the Lord
for he is good.

Father, in deepest joy
for the love you have shown us,
we ask you to accept our prayers
through Jesus Christ, our Lord.
Amen.

The living God

Father, renew and deepen the faith of your people;
enable us to spread your good news
by our word and our lives.
Silence for prayer
Living God,
we worship you.

Father, breathe your peace into the violence
of our world;
we long for your kingdom to come.
Silence for prayer
Living God,
we worship you.

Father, refresh and soothe
all our scratchy and worn relationships;
fill our homes with your love.
Silence for prayer
Living God,
we worship you.

Father, comfort and reassure
all those who are suffering;
heal them to wholeness.
Silence for prayer
Living God,
we worship you.

Father, have mercy on those who draw close to death;
make us all aware of your abiding presence.

Silence for prayer

Living God,
we worship you.

Father, awaken us to see again the wonder
and delight of life;
fill us with thankfulness.

Silence for prayer

Living God,
we worship you
and ask you to accept our prayers
for the sake of Jesus Christ, your Son.
Amen.

Holy God

Holy God, we come to plead for the Church
in its weakness and lack of unity;
may we be one as you are one.

Silence for prayer

Holy God,
we trust in your goodness.

Holy God, we come to plead for our world
in its confusion and injustices.

Silence for prayer

Holy God,
we trust in your goodness.

Holy God, we come to plead for our families
and friends
in their needs and difficulties.

Silence for prayer

Holy God,
we trust in your goodness.

Holy God, we come to plead for those who suffer
in their pain and weariness.

Silence for prayer

Holy God,
we trust in your goodness.

Holy God, we come to plead for the dying
and the bereaved
in their grief and loneliness.
Silence for prayer
Holy God,
we trust in your goodness.

Holy God, we come to plead for the coming
of your kingdom
in every place and in every person.
Silence for prayer
We thank you, Father,
that your holiness
is full of mercy and compassion.
**Accept these prayers
for the sake of Jesus, our Saviour.
Amen.**

The glory of God's love

Father, wherever your Church has become short-sighted,
inattentive or inflexible,
work in your healing love.
Silence for prayer
Lord, awaken us
to notice your glory.

Father, wherever our nations have lost their way,
their sense of human worth or their integrity,
nourish them with your love.
Silence for prayer
Lord, awaken us
to notice your glory.

Father, wherever our relationships are fragmented,
or shallow or offensive to you,
challenge us with your love.
Silence for prayer
Lord, awaken us
to notice your glory.

Father, wherever people are suffering,
whether physically, mentally or emotionally,
comfort them with your love.
Silence for prayer
Lord, awaken us
to notice your glory.

Father, wherever people are fearful of death,
or anxious for the future,
reassure them with your love.

Silence for prayer

Lord, awaken us
to notice your glory.

Father, wherever your will is being fulfilled,
or hearts are learning to trust your love,
we join you in your joy.

Silence for prayer

Open our eyes, Father,
to the light of your glory
in the world you have made,
in the people around us
and in the face of Jesus Christ, our Lord.
Amen.

God knows us and loves us

Father, we bring to your healing love
our shallowness of faith,
our need for your grace and power
in the Church throughout the world.
Silence for prayer

You know us completely
and love us for ever.

We bring to your healing love
our need for your serenity and wisdom
in the governments of all the nations.
Silence for prayer

You know us completely
and love us for ever.

We bring to your healing love
our need of patience, mutual affection
and forgiveness
in our homes and families.
Silence for prayer

You know us completely
and love us for ever.

We bring to your healing love
the injured and broken-hearted,
the weak and the frightened.
Silence for prayer

You know us completely
and love us for ever.

We bring to your healing love
those whom death has released from pain,
and those in great sorrow at losing loved ones.
Silence for prayer
You know us completely
and love us for ever.

We bring you our thanks and praise
for all that is good and hopeful and positive,
all that is redeemed from suffering.
Silence for prayer
Father,
trusting in your great love for us,
we bring you these prayers
in the name of Jesus, your Son.
Amen.

GOD IS
OUR STRENGTH

Strong in the strength of the Lord

We pray for all missionaries and evangelists,
particularly those who are ridiculed or persecuted
for their faith;
we pray for all who hear your word,
that they may receive it with joy.
Silence for prayer

In your strength, Lord,
make us strong.

We pray for those in local, national
and international government;
for integrity and sensitivity in all debates;
for right judgements, good counsel and fair laws.
Silence for prayer

In your strength, Lord,
make us strong.

We pray for our homes and all who live or visit there;
that each room may be blessed with your love
to nurture forgiveness, mutual respect and compassion.
Silence for prayer

In your strength, Lord,
make us strong.

We pray for those whose bodies are weak,
whose minds are blurred, whose spirits are listless;
we pray for comfort, healing, refreshment and peace.
Silence for prayer

In your strength, Lord,
make us strong.

We pray for those whose life on earth has ended,
that you will welcome them with mercy
into your kingdom;
we pray for those who have died violently
and for those who struggle to forgive.
Silence for prayer

In your strength, Lord,
make us strong.

We pray for the truth of your astounding love
to reach deeper into our understanding as we praise
and bless your name in our lives.
Silence for prayer

Father, we bring you these prayers
and ask that we may live
in the strength of Jesus Christ,
in whose name we pray.
Amen.

Leaning on God

Father, we lean on your love as we pray
for your Church – collectively,
and as a mixed bag of individuals,
with needs, disappointments and fears.

Silence for prayer

In all things, Father,
we pray your kingdom in.

We lean on your wisdom as we pray
for local, national and international leaders,
subject to pressures and conflicting values.

Silence for prayer

In all things, Father,
we pray your kingdom in.

We lean on your affectionate understanding
as we pray for our homes and all homes in this area,
with their expectations and misunderstandings,
their security and insecurity.

Silence for prayer

In all things, Father,
we pray your kingdom in.

We lean on your compassion as we pray
for all who are hurting in body, mind or spirit.

Silence for prayer

In all things, Father,
we pray your kingdom in.

We lean on your faithfulness as we pray
for those who have died, and those who mourn.
Silence for prayer
In all things, Father,
we pray your kingdom in.

We lean on your accepting love as we pray
in thankfulness for all you are doing in our lives,
and all you have in mind for us in the future.
Silence for prayer
Father, we bring you
not only our prayers
but our lives
to be used in the service of your kingdom,
through Jesus Christ, our Lord.
Amen.

We put our trust in God

We call to mind all who are insulted
or persecuted for their faith;
all who speak out
and those who are afraid to.

Silence for prayer

Help us, O Lord:
we put our trust in you.

We call to mind those working for peace,
justice and hope in an aching world.

Silence for prayer

Help us, O Lord:
we put our trust in you.

We call to mind those whose lives
are bound up with ours;
we remember all the families and streets
represented here.

Silence for prayer

Help us, O Lord:
we put our trust in you.

We call to mind those whose bodies
battle against disease or pain;
those whose minds battle against confusion
and depression.

Silence for prayer

Help us, O Lord:
we put our trust in you.

We call to mind those who are dying
in fear or loneliness;
those who have recently passed into eternity.

Silence for prayer

Help us, O Lord:
we put our trust in you.

We call to mind the ways we have been helped
through difficult times,
and have grown to understand more
of your loving care.
And we commend the rest of our life to your keeping.

Silence for prayer

Father, trusting in your love,
we lay these prayers before you,
in the name of Jesus Christ.
Amen.

God our refuge

Father, we pray for all whose Christian ministry
brings hardship and persecution.
Silence for prayer
Keep us safe, O God:
for in you we take refuge.

Father, we pray for all in positions of power
and responsibility,
and those negotiating for peace.
Silence for prayer
Keep us safe, O God:
for in you we take refuge.

Father, we pray for those amongst whom
we live and work,
for our friends and all whom we value.
Silence for prayer
Keep us safe, O God:
for in you we take refuge.

Father, we pray for all who feel
overwhelmed with troubles,
and all who are mentally or physically impaired.
Silence for prayer
Keep us safe, O God:
for in you we take refuge.

Father, we pray for those who are fearful
or superstitious,
and those who long to believe in your reality.

Silence for prayer

Keep us safe, O God:
for in you we take refuge.

Father, we thank you for all you have taught us
and all you are teaching us in our lives
at the moment.

Silence for prayer

Lord God, we put our trust in you,
who made us and redeemed us,
through Jesus Christ, our Lord.
Amen.

Safe in the love of God

Father, into your care we commit all Christians,
all in ministry and all church leaders.
Silence for prayer
O Lord, our God,
it is good to be safe in your love.

Father, into your care we commit our world,
with its needs and failures,
hope and despair.
Silence for prayer
O Lord, our God,
it is good to be safe in your love.

Father, into your care we commit those we love,
and those we could love more.
Silence for prayer
O Lord, our God,
it is good to be safe in your love.

Father, into your care we commit those of all ages
who are in danger,
and live in fear.
Silence for prayer
O Lord, our God,
it is good to be safe in your love.

Father, into your care we commit
those who have recently died
and all who mourn for them.

Silence for prayer

O Lord, our God,
it is good to be safe in your love.

Father, we rejoice in the way you look after us,
and thank you for providing for all our needs.

Silence for prayer

Heavenly Father,
our help in times of need,
accept these prayers
for the sake of your Son,
Jesus Christ, our Lord.
Amen.

Our God is able

We pray for everyone who has never yet
heard of Jesus,
and all those who don't yet know
how much God loves them.
Enable us to use each opportunity
we are given
to show God's love in our behaviour.
Silence for prayer

With God
nothing is impossible!

We pray for the Queen and those who
govern our country;
we ask you to be among them as they
make important decisions.
We bring to you the many problems
that are so difficult to solve lovingly.
Silence for prayer

With God
nothing is impossible!

We pray for all who spend their lives
feeling dissatisfied;
for those who are unhappy, lonely or overworked.
We ask you to lift their spirits
and give them peace and joy.
Silence for prayer

With God
nothing is impossible!

We pray for those in pain
and those whose peaceful lives
have suddenly been shattered.
Help them gather the fragments to start again;
give courage and hope.

Silence for prayer

With God
nothing is impossible!

Lord, we thank you that your grace
is sufficient for us,
no matter what happens to us.
In a time of silence in God's company,
let us thank him for his many blessings.

Silence for prayer

God of great power and love,
we cast all our care on you,
in the name of Jesus,
Saviour, Lord and Friend.
Amen.

God's power is made perfect in weakness

Fellow members of Christ,
let us approach our heavenly Father,
acknowledging the wonder of his involvement with us,
and asking him to help us.

We pray for all who labour to spread the good news,
especially those who face threatening behaviour,
imprisonment or persecution;
for those who are tempted to remain silent
in order to avoid danger to themselves or their families;
that they may be given your courage and your peace.
Silence for prayer

Lord, in our weakness,
we ask for your help.

We pray for all the injustice, cruelty
and oppression of our world;
its confusion of priorities,
its lost opportunities and misdirected zeal;
that we may be guided unceasingly
by the level-headed, compassionate leadership
of God's Spirit.
Silence for prayer

Lord, in our weakness,
we ask for your help.

We pray for our families, friends and neighbours;
for the very young and the very old in our care;
for wisdom to see opportunities of Christ's love,
and for enough energy and time
to do what God needs us to.

Silence for prayer

Lord, in our weakness,
we ask for your help.

We pray for all who are wounded and injured –
those in hospital and all in pain;
that they may find Christ among them
in their suffering.
We pray for those who inflict pain on others;
for terrorists, murderers
and all who are fired with hatred;
that their lives may be transformed
by encountering Christ.

Silence for prayer

Lord, in our weakness,
we ask for your help.

We pray for those on the verge of death
and those who have passed into eternity;
may they rest in your peace for ever.
We give you thanks for all your care and healing love.

Silence for prayer

Lord, you are our strength in times of weakness;
accept these prayers
for the sake of Jesus Christ, our Saviour.
Amen.

A VERY PRESENT
HELP IN TROUBLE

Deliver us from evil

Companions in Christ,
knowing that our heavenly Father
has sufficient grace for all our needs,
let us pray to him now.

Lord, we pray for the leaders and ministers
of your Church, especially those for whom
your work has brought danger and persecution;
may they never lose sight of your presence,
which comforts and protects.

Silence for prayer

Lord of power,
deliver us from evil.

We pray for clear light and guidance as our world faces
the problems and crises of another week;
for the willingness of leaders
to be wisely advised and courageous
in doing what is right.

Silence for prayer

Lord of power,
deliver us from evil.

We pray for a greater willingness in us
to live and work in your strength;
for a deepening trust in your power
to save, heal and overcome temptation.

Silence for prayer

Lord of power,
deliver us from evil.

We pray for all addicted to drugs,
alcohol, solvent abuse, violence,
or any other habit that enslaves;
for all victims of war, and abuse;
for the terrified and the suicidal.

Silence for prayer

Lord of power,
deliver us from evil.

We pray that all who have passed from this life
may live in the joy of your presence for ever.

Silence for prayer

Lord of all power,
deliver us from evil.

Thank you, Father, for all the evils
that have been conquered,
and all the good that is done through your power
every day throughout our world.
Help us to notice your goodness.

Silence for prayer

Father, we bring these prayers
trusting in the power of your love,
which you have shown to us
in Jesus Christ, our Lord.
Amen.

Looking for God's help

Companions in Christ, as we remember with gratitude
all that God has done for us,
let us bring to his love the needs and concerns
of the Church and of the world.

We bring to your love, Lord,
the daily work of each member of Christ's body;
that in constant prayer we may learn your will
and your way of doing things,
until we work exclusively for your glory.
Silence for prayer

In you we trust:
we look to you for help.

We bring to your love, Lord,
the mistakes, short-sightedness
and arrogance of our world;
that in Christ we may learn to respect one another
and the treasures of the planet we inhabit.
Silence for prayer

In you we trust:
we look to you for help.

We bring to your love, Lord,
the wounded and the afraid,
the despairing and the rejected;
that they may find Christ suffering alongside them
and allow him to restore them to wholeness.
Silence for prayer

In you we trust:
we look to you for help.

We bring to your love, Lord,
our busy concern with unimportant things;
that in spending more time in Christ's company
we may learn to act and react in all our relationships
with the character and Spirit of Jesus.

Silence for prayer

In you we trust:
we look to you for help.

We bring to your love, Lord,
all our dear ones who are separated
from us through death;
that as children of eternity we may always
remember how close they are,
linked by your eternal love.

Silence for prayer

In you we trust:
we look to you for help.

Almighty Father, hear the prayers we offer,
and use our bodies, minds and spirits
in establishing your kingdom.

Silence for prayer

Lord, give us the faith
to know that you are near
and ready to answer our prayers
for the sake of Jesus, your Son.
Amen.

Cast all your cares upon him

My brothers and sisters in Christ,
knowing the deep love that surrounds us
and reaches out to us in every distress,
let us unload our burdens of care
to the healing power of our heavenly Father.

We bring before you the Church's work
among the homeless, the disillusioned
and the apathetic,
in communities all over the world.
Silence for prayer
Life-giving Lord,
hear us and help us, we pray.

We bring before you all areas of the world
where lack of communication
breeds suspicion and fear;
where lack of understanding
breeds insecurity and a spirit of revenge.
Silence for prayer
Life-giving Lord,
hear us and help us, we pray.

We bring before you each member of this community,
each individual anxiety and sorrow,
each hope and dream,
each weakness and special need.
Silence for prayer
Life-giving Lord,
hear us and help us, we pray.

We bring before you all whose lives are crippled
by unrepented sin or the refusal to forgive;
all whose lives are constantly restless
and devoid of peace.

Silence for prayer

Life-giving Lord,
hear us and help us, we pray.

We bring before you those who have died
and those who miss them.

Silence for prayer

Life-giving Lord,
hear us and help us, we pray.

We bring before you the joy and happiness
of our daily life,
the blessings that lift our hearts to praise you.

Silence for prayer

Lord, in these our prayers
we share our concerns with you.
Give us the faith to know
that you hear and answer,
through Jesus Christ, your Son.
Amen.

Trusting God to help us

In the Spirit of Jesus Christ, our brother,
let us draw near to our heavenly Father
and pray to him together.

We pray for all who labour in the painstaking work
of building up the kingdom of heaven;
guide them in uncertainty,
encourage them in apparent failure,
and train them in trust through perseverance.

Silence for prayer

Father of great mercy,
we trust you to help us.

We pray for the leaders of our country
and of all peoples throughout the world;
for newspaper editors, film directors
and all who influence our nation through the media;
may our world be led to understand your values,
and know your peace.

Silence for prayer

Father of great mercy,
we trust you to help us.

We pray for those we rely on and those who rely on us;
for an increase of loyalty and trust;
for guidance in the way we use
our time, money and abilities;
for courage to commit our lives to you more deeply.

Silence for prayer

Father of great mercy,
we trust you to help us.

We pray for those who have lost their way in life,
and long to be rescued and loved back to wholeness;
for those suffering through illness
or handicap or accident.

Silence for prayer

Father of great mercy,
we trust you to help us.

We pray for those who have passed
through the gateway of death into eternity;
may they abide in your peace for ever.

Silence for prayer

Father of great mercy,
we trust you to help us.

We thank you for the many blessings of life
which you give us each day;
for the wonder of your creation
and the joy and comfort of your presence.

Silence for prayer

Loving Father, hear our prayers
and use us in your answering,
through Jesus Christ, our Lord.
Amen.

Keep us in your love

My Christian sisters and brothers,
as we rejoice at being called
and chosen by our heavenly Father,
let us speak with him of our needs and concerns.

Father, we commend to your love
all leaders and teachers in the Church;
that in all they do and say they may stay close to you,
alert to your will and constantly prepared
to move forward where you guide.
Silence for prayer

Father, hear us:
keep us in your love.

We commend to your love
all talks and negotiations in industry
and in matters of international concern;
that they may be marked by generosity of spirit,
and a desire for reconciliation that comes only from you.
Silence for prayer

Father, hear us:
keep us in your love.

We commend to your love
all who are especially precious to us,
and all with whom we find it difficult to relate;
that we may always treat one another
with Christlike love.
Silence for prayer

Father, hear us:
keep us in your love.

We commend to your love
all outsiders and outcasts,
all who have been rejected by their family
or their country;
that rifts may be healed, relationships repaired
and new bonds of love forged in Christ.
Silence for prayer
Father, hear us:
keep us in your love.

We commend to your love
those who have reached the end
of their journey on earth;
welcome them into your heavenly kingdom
and bring us, too, at death, safely home.

Heavenly Father, with you beside us
our journey is so richly blessed with joy and peace;
how can we ever thank you
for the generosity of your love and ceaseless care!
Silence for prayer
Father, with these prayers
we give our lives into your keeping,
through Jesus Christ, our Lord.
Amen.

God our saviour

In the Spirit of Jesus Christ, who can save us from sin,
let us pray to our heavenly Father
for the Church and for the world.

We pray for all who witness to the truth of saving love,
especially those whose Christian witness
brings danger, hardship or ridicule.
Silence for prayer
Father of love,
we believe and trust in you.

We pray for our Queen and all who hold
positions of authority in our world;
that they may be led to right and just decisions
in keeping with your will.
Silence for prayer
Father of love,
we believe and trust in you.

We pray for the members of our families,
for all those who are precious to us
and those we find difficult to get on with;
strengthen our love for one another
and give us the grace to forgive wholeheartedly.
Silence for prayer
Father of love,
we believe and trust in you.

We pray for the vulnerable and the frightened,
for those tormented by guilt and those who despair;
give them the comfort of knowing you are with them
and draw them to the light of your forgiveness.

Silence for prayer

Father of love,
we believe and trust in you.

We pray for those who have died
and for those who mourn;
grant them peace in your presence for ever.

Silence for prayer

Father of love,
we believe and trust in you.

Thank you, Father, for supplying us always
with the strength we need to do your will,
and for the joy of working with you.

Silence for prayer

Father, deepen our faith
that we may always trust in you,
through Jesus Christ, our Lord.
Amen.

God works in all things for our good

Father, we pray for the Church
and all Christians in their various callings;
we remember the conflicts and divisions,
and the movement towards unity.

Silence for prayer

Lord, we believe
that in all things you work for our good.

We pray for those who have been given
great responsibility in this world.

Silence for prayer

Lord, we believe
that in all things you work for our good.

We pray for our parents
and all who have influenced our thinking.

Silence for prayer

Lord, we believe
that in all things you work for our good.

We pray for those in great need,
financially, emotionally or physically.

Silence for prayer

Lord, we believe
that in all things you work for our good.

We pray for those whose earthly journey
has come to an end;
and we pray for those who feel empty
without their physical company.

Silence for prayer

Lord, we believe
that in all things you work for our good.

We praise and thank you, Father,
that we can trust you with our lives
both in darkness and in light,
in sorrow and in joy,
in the strength of Jesus Christ,
our Saviour, Companion and Friend.
Amen.

Lord, have mercy on all who suffer

We call to mind our brothers and sisters in Christ
who are imprisoned or suffering persecution
simply for believing what we believe.

Silence for prayer

Trust in the Lord
for with the Lord there is mercy.

We call to mind those whose lives
are caught up in war, political unrest,
family feuds or nationalistic grievances.

Silence for prayer

Trust in the Lord
for with the Lord there is mercy.

We call to mind refugees and all who do not know
whether their loved ones are safe or not;
all whose homes are places of violence
and all whose homes are havens of love.

Silence for prayer

Trust in the Lord
for with the Lord there is mercy.

We call to mind those imprisoned by guilt,
addiction or bitterness;
and all those who undergo suffering bravely
and bring joy to those who care for them.

Silence for prayer

Trust in the Lord
for with the Lord there is mercy.

We call to mind those who have recently died
and those who miss them;
those who are nearing death,
and those who support them.

Silence for prayer

Trust in the Lord
for with the Lord there is mercy.

We call to mind the times when God
has carried us through difficulties,
and thank him for his faithful love.

Silence for prayer

Lord, we entrust to your love
those we remember in our prayers,
through Jesus Christ, our Lord.
Amen.

In the pressures of life

Let us bring to God our loving Father
all the cares that weigh on our hearts,
knowing that he understands us
better than we understand ourselves.

Father, we bring the daily work
of those who labour to spread the good news of Christ
amid apathy, ridicule or prejudice;
may they be encouraged and strengthened.
Silence for prayer
Father, hear us
and prepare us to meet you.

Father, we bring our daily work,
with all the pressures, monotony,
enjoyment and mistakes;
help your world to recognise your presence
and trust in your love.
Silence for prayer
Father, hear us
and prepare us to meet you.

Father, we bring all our loved ones,
with their hopes and disappointments,
their struggles and their successes;
may they be guided and nurtured by your love.
Silence for prayer

Father, hear us
and prepare us to meet you.

Father, we bring all those
whose lives seem to them bleak,
painful or empty of meaning;
please release them, unburden them,
and fill them with your gift of joy.
Silence for prayer

Father, hear us
and prepare us to meet you.

Father, we commend to your unfailing love
all who have died, especially . . .
Silence for prayer

Father, hear us
and prepare us to meet you.

Filled with thankfulness for all
your many blessings to us,
we offer you our praise.
May we never forget your generosity.
Silence for prayer

Father, you are with us
at the centre of our lives;
**accept our prayers
and help us to live for you,
through Jesus Christ, our Lord.
Amen.**

GOD RENEWS US

You alone can make us whole

Let us approach our heavenly Father in humility,
as we bring to his restoring love
all our concern for the Church and the world.

Lord, we bring to you
the divided Christian community;
lead us tenderly to wholeness and unity.
Silence for prayer
Lord God,
you alone can make us whole.

Lord, we bring to you
the divided world,
split between wealth and poverty,
complacency and oppression;
break through all barriers
with your love and reconciliation.
Silence for prayer
Lord God,
you alone can make us whole.

Lord, we bring to you
the wounds and hurts of our own lives;
and of our families;
all unresolved tensions and sorrows,
all reunions, joys and healing;
bless and renew our lives with your living presence.
Silence for prayer
Lord God,
you alone can make us whole.

Lord, we bring to you
all in pain or distress;
the mentally and physically handicapped
and all whom society prefers to ignore;
may your love nourish and heal, accept and restore.

Silence for prayer

Lord God,
you alone can make us whole.

Lord, we commend to your everlasting
love and care, all who have died, especially . . .

Silence for prayer

With great joy in our hearts
we offer you thanks and praise
for all the gifts and blessings you lavish on us;
may we proclaim our thankfulness by the lives we lead.

Silence for prayer

Father, receive these prayers
which we offer in the name of Jesus Christ, our Lord.
Amen.

Renew our faith

Pray for all those
whose faith is worn or battered,
bringing to mind anyone known to you.
Silence for prayer
For with God
everything is possible.

Pray for a deepening of faith in all church-goers,
particularly those in your own area.
Silence for prayer
For with God
everything is possible.

Pray for our society to be changed
and renewed in God's way,
bringing to mind
the areas that particularly concern you.
Silence for prayer
For with God
everything is possible.

Pray for those who are in pain or anguish
and those who are frightened.
Silence for prayer
For with God
everything is possible.

In a time of silence
we share with God our Father
our personal needs and concerns.
Silence for prayer
For with God
everything is possible.

Thank God for what he is doing in your life,
and for his living presence with us
now and always.
Silence for prayer
Father, enlarge our faith
to see you at work in the world,
to feel you at work in our hearts,
through Jesus Christ, our Lord.
Amen.

God's love restores us

Father, we think of the variety of individuals
who make up your Church;
make us quick to encourage one another
and slow to criticise.

Silence for prayer

Thank you, Lord,
for restoring us through love.

Father, we think of the responsibility we all have
in looking after our world,
and our desperate need for guidance.

Silence for prayer

Thank you, Lord,
for restoring us through love.

Father, we think of the joys and sorrows
among families and friends,
and our need of the grace to forgive one another.

Silence for prayer

Thank you, Lord,
for restoring us through love.

Father, we think of the pain
which so many suffer all over the world,
and of their thirst for comfort and encouragement.

Silence for prayer

Thank you, Lord,
for restoring us through love.

We pray in silence now
for our own particular needs and concerns.

Silence for prayer

Thank you, Lord,
for restoring us through love.

Father, we think of all those who dedicate their lives
to building a better world with you,
and thank you for their faithfulness.

Silence for prayer

Father, accept these prayers,
**and give us the grace
to walk in your love
all our days,
through Jesus Christ, our Lord.
Amen.**

God, make us new

In the chapels, churches and cathedrals,
and in every gathering of Christians,
God all-knowing, God all-loving,
come, make us new.
Silence for prayer

Where faith is frayed,
where prayer is casual,
where God is patronised
and the harvest is ignored,
God all-knowing, God all-loving,
come, make us new.
Silence for prayer

In the homes, shops, schools
and meeting places of our town,
in the conversations we have this week,
God all-knowing, God all-loving,
come, make us new.
Silence for prayer

Where people are sad or burdened with guilt,
where illness and frailty are hard to bear cheerfully,
God all-knowing, God all-loving,
come, make us new.
Silence for prayer

As those we have known and loved
journey from this life into eternity,
and we call to mind that heaven is our home,
God all-knowing, God all-loving,
come, make us new.
Silence for prayer

In our moments and days,
our sorrows and our joys,
God all-knowing, God all-loving,
**come, make us new
and accept these prayers
for the sake of your Son,
our Saviour, Jesus Christ.
Amen.**

Make us more like you

In faith, knowing that where two or three are gathered
in your name you have promised to be among them,
let our minds and hearts be filled
with stillness as we pray.

We pray for the Church;
that all your ministers may be given
perception and understanding,
to lead people into the light of your truth.
Silence for prayer
Lord of glory,
make us more like you.

We pray for all councils, committees and conferences;
that a spirit of integrity may underlie all discussion
and a desire for goodness inspire all decisions.
Silence for prayer
Lord of glory,
make us more like you.

We pray for all families,
especially those who have troubles;
that they may not be damaged through their suffering,
but rather grow in compassion and understanding.
Silence for prayer
Lord of glory,
make us more like you.

We pray for those in pain and distress;
for the mentally, physically and emotionally disabled;
that they may be comforted
and strengthened by your presence,
trusting in your love which never fails.
Silence for prayer
Lord of glory,
make us more like you.

We pray for the dying and those who have
already moved on from this world into eternity;
may they rest for ever in your peace.
Silence for prayer
Lord of glory,
make us more like you.

In thankfulness and praise
we remember all your many blessings,
given to us each day,
and ask you to help us become
more generous-hearted and appreciative.
Silence for prayer
Father, we thank you
for showing yourself to us
in Jesus Christ.
Help us to follow him day by day.
Amen.

Lord, give us new life

Wherever Christians are spiritually dry or brittle,
wherever the loving has lost its freshness,
we pray for refreshment.
Silence for prayer
Father, touch our lives
and give them new life.

Wherever the nations scramble for power and revenge,
wherever materialism dulls the spirit,
we pray for realigned priorities and values.
Silence for prayer
Father, touch our lives
and give them new life.

Wherever homes are disturbed by financial problems,
difficult relationships and long-term illness,
we pray for guidance and support.
Silence for prayer
Father, touch our lives
and give them new life.

Wherever slow recovery makes time hang heavily,
wherever hope and joy are fading,
we pray for encouragement and delight.
Silence for prayer
Father, touch our lives
and give them new life.

Wherever people are dying to this world,
wherever lives are cut short by accidents, war or famine,
we pray for your mercy and words of comfort.
Silence for prayer
Father, touch our lives
and give them new life.

Whether our hearts are light or heavy,
whether the day goes well or not,
we give you praise and proclaim your love.
Silence for prayer
Father and giver of life,
accept not only these prayers
but our very selves,
for the sake of Jesus, our Lord.
Amen.

GOD WITHIN US

Let God's mind and heart be in you

Father, let your light stream into every Christian life
to show up anything that needs cutting out, healing,
renewing, softening or purifying.

Silence for prayer

Help us to think with your mind
and love with your heart.

Father, let your wisdom take control
in all decisions and advice,
all legislation and negotiation.

Silence for prayer

Help us to think with your mind
and love with your heart.

Father, let the warmth of your love
be present in every home
and in every relationship,
in our celebrations and our struggles.

Silence for prayer

Help us to think with your mind
and love with your heart.

Father, let the power of your healing bring to wholeness
those who are disturbed and agitated,
suffering in body or mind or spirit.

Silence for prayer

Help us to think with your mind
and love with your heart.

Father, let your loving mercy bring the dead and dying
safely home to heaven,
and give comfort to those who mourn.

Silence for prayer

Help us to think with your mind
and love with your heart.

Father, let your joy fill our lives
as we delight in living according to your ways,
through Jesus Christ, our Lord.
Amen.

Breathe on us, breath of God

In the presence of God, the giver of all life,
let us lift our hearts and pray.

We pray for all who are training
for ministry in your Church;
may they grow in wisdom and humility,
and be increasingly filled with the life
you have won for us.
Silence for prayer

Lord, breathe into us
that we may live.

We pray for all areas of bureaucracy
which frustrate and delay the course of useful action;
for areas where anarchy undermines stability;
for areas of political corruption;
that whatever is good may flourish and grow,
so evil is rendered powerless and overthrown.
Silence for prayer

Lord, breathe into us
that we may live.

We pray for all who are engaged or newly married;
for those coping with family problems,
difficult circumstances or bereavement;
may they lean on your loving presence
which dispels all fear, and brings life and peace.

Silence for prayer

Lord, breathe into us
that we may live.

We pray that your calming reassurance
will bring peace of mind and spirit
to those worried about the future,
those dreading some difficult event,
and those who are frightened of dying.

Silence for prayer

Lord, breathe into us
that we may live.

We thank you for the life and example
of all who have lived, worked and died
in the joy of your service;
may we one day share with them
eternal life in your presence.

Silence for prayer

Lord, breathe into us
that we may live.

Father, with thankful hearts we offer ourselves
to be used wherever you need us.
Accept these prayers
for the sake of Jesus Christ.
Amen.

Touch our lives that we may live

Let us pray, my brothers and sisters,
in the knowledge of our Father's infinite mercy.

We pray for all Christian people and Church leaders;
all whose faith is battered through disaster or suffering;
may we know the certainty of your abiding presence
which transforms and rebuilds.
Silence for prayer
Touch our lives, Lord,
that we may live.

We pray for all world leaders,
all administrative bodies and political institutions;
may they be always aware
of the real needs of those they serve
and be effective in providing for them.
Silence for prayer
Touch our lives, Lord,
that we may live.

We pray for our local community,
for our families and our friends,
with all the hopes, fears, problems and needs;
make us ready to serve you in our own area
and spread your life-giving joy.
Silence for prayer
Touch our lives, Lord,
that we may live.

We pray for the dying
and those who love and tend them;
for the bereaved and desolate;
may all in trouble and sorrow
draw strength from your life
and your victory over death.

Silence for prayer

Touch our lives, Lord,
that we may live.

We pray for those who have died
that, falling asleep to this life,
they may wake to eternal life
in the joy of heaven.

Silence for prayer

We thank you, heavenly Father,
for saving us from sin's destruction
and making it possible to live
in such abundant fullness.

Silence for prayer

Father, we offer these prayers
in the name of Jesus Christ, our Lord.
Amen.

Filled with the love of God

My friends in Christ,
mindful of God's steadfast love for us,
let us pray to our heavenly Father.

We pray for faithfulness among all Christians,
particularly when conflicts arise
between Christian values and social expectations;
for a drawing together towards unity
and an increase of the kind of caring
that should make Christ's followers stand out.
Silence for prayer
Father, live in us:
fill us with love.

We pray for all factories, mines, quarries,
all processing and refining plants
and all who work in them or live close by;
may they be safely and responsibly managed
with industrial relations based on mutual respect,
courtesy and goodwill.
Silence for prayer
Father, live in us:
fill us with love.

We pray for everyone who has helped us
and forgiven us this week
at home, work or school;
for anyone in need whom we could help;
make us more prepared to take the initiative
in caring for others, and taking ourselves less seriously.

Silence for prayer

Father, live in us:
fill us with love.

We pray for the malnourished and starving,
the grief-stricken and the bereaved;
for the homeless, and those surviving in inadequate
accommodation;
open our eyes to see Christ among all who suffer,
so we are inspired to spend our lives
in helping those in need.
Silence for prayer

Father, live in us:
fill us with love.

We pray for those who have died;
that falling asleep to pain and suffering
they may wake to the joy and freedom of your heaven.
Silence for prayer

Lord, your glory is everywhere for us to see,
and we thank you for all the love
that brightens our world.
Silence for prayer

Father of love,
accept these prayers
for the sake of your Son,
our Saviour, Jesus Christ.
Amen.

Filled with the fullness of God

We pray that your Church will have courage
to speak up for what is right and loving;
we pray for those who are persecuted
or imprisoned because of their faith.

Silence for prayer

Father, fill us up
with goodness and with love.

We pray for integrity and wisdom
in all who advise and lead in our world;
we pray for the areas where law and order
have broken down.

Silence for prayer

Father, fill us up
with goodness and with love.

We pray that our homes may be places of welcome,
comfort and friendship;
we pray for all who will walk in and out
of our homes this week.

Silence for prayer

Father, fill us up
with goodness and with love.

We pray for all who are victims of greed,
cruelty and revenge;
we pray for those who hate,
and all who are finding it difficult to forgive.

Silence for prayer

Father, fill us up
with goodness and with love.

We pray for those who have come to the end
of their earthly life,
and those who mourn.

Silence for prayer

Father, fill us up
with goodness and with love.

We praise and bless you
for every scrap of tenderness,
every spark of joy,
and every glimpse of your glory.

Silence for prayer

Good and loving Father,
accept these prayers
for the sake of your Son,
our Saviour, Jesus Christ.
Amen.

Let the light of God shine through us

My friends in Christ,
let us pray to our heavenly Father
trusting in his generous mercy.

We pray for the Church
as it witnesses to Christ in the world;
may its members be always aware
that they are called to be servants,
ready and happy to minister
to the spiritual, emotional and physical needs
of all people.
Silence for prayer
Lord of light,
shine through our lives.

We pray for the leaders of every community and nation;
may governments reflect the values
of responsible caring, compassion and integrity,
so that no individual or minority group
is abused or left in need.
Silence for prayer
Lord of light,
shine through our lives.

We pray for a breaking down of any complacency
or blindness in us
until we are able to see the needs around us,
and can work in your strength,
giving our whole lives away
in loving those whom you love.
Silence for prayer

Lord of light,
shine through our lives.

We pray for the rejected, neglected,
shunned or despised;
for the unwanted and the disturbed;
for the ill and the injured;
may they be healed, restored and comforted.
Silence for prayer

Lord of light,
shine through our lives.

We pray for those who have passed
through the gateway of death into eternity;
may they know the joy of your presence for ever.
Silence for prayer

We offer you our thanks
for every opportunity we are given
to witness to your unfailing love;
may our words and our lives proclaim your glory,
through Jesus Christ, our Lord.
Amen.

JESUS CHRIST, OUR LORD

The coming of Christ

My brothers and sisters in Christ,
as we watch together for his coming,
let us pray together for the Church and for the world.

Lord, strengthen and guide your Church
in its mission to the world;
that sinners may be alerted to repentance
and many may be brought to the joy
of living in your love.

Silence for prayer

Lord, come to us:
live in us now.

Lord, we pray for the whole created world
and its peoples;
that no evil may thwart your will,
but that rather your kingdom may be established
and your will done.

Silence for prayer

Lord, come to us:
live in us now.

Lord, bless this community
and all who serve it;
that we may strive each day to align our lives
with the life of Christ who saves us from sin.

Silence for prayer

Lord, come to us:
live in us now.

Lord, we pray for all who suffer –
mentally, physically and spiritually;
for those who see no further than
immediate, material comforts,
and do not realise their spiritual poverty.

Silence for prayer

Lord, come to us:
live in us now.

We commend to your love
all who have completed their life on earth,
that they may rest in your peace
and share your risen life.

Silence for prayer

Lord, come to us:
live in us now.

Thank you, Lord,
for the richness of your companionship;
for the joy and peace your constant presence gives.

Silence for prayer

Lord, we bring these prayers
in the name of Jesus Christ, your Son.
Amen.

Christ is born today

We pray for all the groups of Christians
who are celebrating Christ's birth today.
Silence for prayer
O God, we thank you
for loving us so much.

We pray for all babies,
that they may be given love and care.
Silence for prayer
O God, we thank you
for loving us so much.

We pray for all who are missing their loved ones,
and all who find Christmas difficult.
Silence for prayer
O God, we thank you
for loving us so much.

We pray for all those in pain
and those with debilitating illness.
Silence for prayer
O God, we thank you
for loving us so much.

We pray for those in prison
and for their families.
Silence for prayer
O God, we thank you
for loving us so much.

We pray for the homeless,
and all refugees.

Silence for prayer

O God, we thank you
for loving us so much.

We thank you for the joy of Christmas
and welcome you in our homes.

Silence for prayer

Father,
accept these prayers
for the sake of your Son,
our Saviour, Jesus Christ.
Amen.

Jesus the king of glory

Trusting in Christ's victory over all evil,
let us pray to the Father
for the world and the Church.

We pray for all who witness to Christ
in spite of danger and persecution;
all who work to bring others to know and love you;
that in your strength they may be blessed,
encouraged and bear much fruit.

Silence for prayer

King of glory,
reign in our hearts.

We pray for those who have never received
the good news of your saving love;
for those areas where violence and terrorism
make normal life impossible;
that the spirit of Jesus, the Prince of Peace,
may filter through to increase love
and understanding, respect and goodwill.

Silence for prayer

King of glory,
reign in our hearts.

We pray for our families
and those with whom we live and work;
for particular needs known to us personally;
that in everything we do,
and every minute we live,
your name may be glorified
and your will be done.

Silence for prayer
King of glory,
reign in our hearts.

We pray for the sick and the dying;
that their trust in you may deepen
until their fears are calmed
and they can look forward with real hope
to meeting their Saviour face to face.
Silence for prayer
King of glory,
reign in our hearts.

We pray for those who have died;
may they wake to the joy of eternal life with you.
Silence for prayer
King of glory,
reign in our hearts.

We offer you thanks and praise
for your constant love and kindness,
and especially for the joy of your salvation.
Accept these prayers
for the sake of Jesus Christ, our Lord.
Amen.

The light of the nations

Fellow travellers of Christ's way,
let us pray together
for the Church and for the world.

Father, may our Christian witness,
in a confused and nervous world,
shine with a piercing integrity and warmth
that awakens people's hearts to the love of their Creator.

Silence for prayer

Light of the nations,
shine in our lives.

Bless and protect all travellers and pilgrims;
teach us to cherish the beauty of our world
and share its riches.

Silence for prayer

Light of the nations,
shine in our lives.

Help us to see Christ in the eyes of all those we meet,
and delight in giving you glory
by serving others without expecting rewards.

Silence for prayer

Light of the nations,
shine in our lives.

Direct our vision to see
the best practical ways of providing
shelter for the homeless,
safe accommodation for those who live in fear of violence,
and food for the hungry.
Silence for prayer
Light of the nations,
shine in our lives.

May all who have died in faith
be bathed in the everlasting light
of your loving presence,
and may those who mourn be comforted.
Silence for prayer
Light of the nations,
shine in our lives.

In thankfulness, Father,
we offer you our lives.
Silence for prayer
May the light which we see in Jesus
shine through us
for his name's sake.
Amen.

The resurrection and the life

Filled with the hope and joy of the resurrection,
let us pray confidently to our loving Father.

We pray for the newly baptised and their families;
for those who are sensing God's call
and need reassurance in it;
for all God's people in every part of the world.
Silence for prayer
Life-giving Lord,
reign in our hearts.

We pray for the areas in which there is fighting,
unrest and unresolved conflict;
for the unprincipled, the corrupt
and those who thirst for revenge.
Silence for prayer
Life-giving Lord,
reign in our hearts.

We pray for our neighbours here,
in our street, and at school and at work;
for those with whom we live;
for any who may be wishing
they knew someone willing to be friendly
and share their burden.
Silence for prayer
Life-giving Lord,
reign in our hearts.

We pray for those finding life very trying
and difficult at the moment;
for those who are coping with personal tragedy,
heartache or mourning;
for all who are ill or frail.
Silence for prayer
Life-giving Lord,
reign in our hearts.

We pray for all who have died;
that they may rise to eternal life in the light of heaven.
Silence for prayer
Life-giving Lord,
reign in our hearts.

Father, in so many ways we have been richly blessed;
give us thankful hearts and make us more appreciative
of all that is good in life.
Silence for prayer
We ask these things in the name of Jesus,
the resurrection and the life.
Amen.

THE KINGDOM OF GOD

Your kingdom come

As sons and daughters of our heavenly King,
let us ask our Father's blessing
on the Church and on the world.

We pray for the work of Christ's body, the Church;
that all may labour zealously
for the establishment of your kingdom on earth;
till the world is flooded
with your peace, joy and love.
Silence for prayer

Lord, our heavenly Father,
may your kingdom come.

We pray for the work of all peacemakers,
all who work for justice, reconciliation and harmony;
that you, Lord God of peace and love,
will bless, support and encourage them.
Silence for prayer

Lord, our heavenly Father,
may your kingdom come.

We pray for our own work in this life;
that we may dedicate our energies and resources
more fully to your will,
undertaking every task and activity joyfully,
trusting in your strength.
Silence for prayer

Lord, our heavenly Father,
may your kingdom come.

We pray for the work of those who heal
and tend the sick, the injured and the dying;
for all in their care;
for all involved in medical research
and those whose lives depend on drugs,
dialysis or chemotherapy.

Silence for prayer

Lord, our heavenly Father,
may your kingdom come.

We pray for all who have passed
through the gate of death to eternity;
may they live for ever in your heaven.

Silence for prayer

Lord, our heavenly Father,
may your kingdom come.

We rejoice for all the wonder
and beauty of your creation;
in the constant miracle of life and renewal;
in your amazing and undeserved love
and affection for us.

Silence for prayer

Father,
**accept these prayers which we ask
in the name of Jesus, our King.
Amen.**

The Lord our hope

As sons and daughters of our heavenly Father,
let us pray together, trusting in his love.

We pray that the Church and all its members
may not be stagnant, but flow forward
in the direction you want it to go;
may the Christian hope burn brightly
in our lives and may your kingdom come.

Silence for prayer

Lord, you are our hope:
we believe and trust in you.

We pray that we may all tend and care
for the world you have given us to live in;
may we share its food and riches,
and use them wisely and safely
without waste or destruction.

Silence for prayer

Lord, you are our hope:
we believe and trust in you.

We pray for the sick, the injured and the distressed;
for the dying and for those who mourn;
may your healing presence
bring wholeness and comfort.

Silence for prayer

Lord, you are our hope:
we believe and trust in you.

We pray for our own circle of family and friends;
for personal spiritual growth;
may we be more watchful,
preparing ourselves more thoroughly
day by day to meet you face to face.

Silence for prayer

Lord, you are our hope:
we believe and trust in you.

We pray for those who have died in faith
and live with you in glory;
may we one day share with them
the joy of being in your presence for ever.

Silence for prayer

Lord, you are our hope:
we believe and trust in you.

We thank you, Father,
for all your goodness and kindness to us;
for the hope of heaven and the comfort of your love.

Silence for prayer

Lord of all hopefulness,
**accept these prayers
for the sake of Jesus Christ.
Amen.**

The love of God at work

Father, work your love in the Church,
her ministers and all her members,
particularly where there is any hardness of heart,
or misunderstanding of your will.

Silence for prayer

Lord, we know and believe
that you will keep us safe.

Father, work your love in our world,
guiding our leaders and redeeming good
from all that is evil.

Silence for prayer

Lord, we know and believe
that you will keep us safe.

Father, work your love in our homes,
making them places of welcome,
understanding and forgiveness.

Silence for prayer

Lord, we know and believe
that you will keep us safe.

Father, work your love in all areas of pain and illness,
anxiety and imprisonment.

Silence for prayer

Lord, we know and believe
that you will keep us safe.

Father, work your love in all areas of sadness
and loneliness,
hopelessness and doubt.
Silence for prayer
Lord, we know and believe
that you will keep us safe.

Father, work your love in all that is beautiful,
all that is growing,
and all that touches our hearts with joy.
Silence for prayer
Father, we trust in you,
and ask these prayers
in the name of Jesus Christ, our Lord.
Amen.

Work your will in our lives

Let us pray together for the leaders
of the Churches
and for the spiritual growth
of all Christians.
Silence for prayer
Father, in you we trust:
work your will in our lives.

Let us pray for the areas of our world
where there is oppression and violence,
pleading for peace and justice.
Silence for prayer
Father, in you we trust:
work your will in our lives.

Let us pray for our home life,
for all the members of our families;
and for those who live
in our neighbourhood.
Silence for prayer
Father, in you we trust:
work your will in our lives.

Let us pray for those who feel imprisoned
by bad health or some kind of disability.
Silence for prayer
Father, in you we trust:
work your will in our lives.

Let us remember those who have died –
those known personally to us
and those we have heard about –
and pray for all who are torn apart by grief.

Silence for prayer

Father, in you we trust:
work your will in our lives.

Let us give thanks for all that is good
and honest, loving and refreshing.

Silence for prayer

Lord, hear our prayers,
which we ask
in the name of Jesus.
Amen.

Learning the ways of God

Father, breathe your spirit of life
into all the members of your Church;
keep us open to your word
and sensitive to your will.

Silence for prayer

All-knowing God,
teach us your ways.

Father, breathe your spirit of counsel
into every debate and international conference;
alert us to act with responsibility and integrity.

Silence for prayer

All-knowing God,
teach us your ways.

Father, breathe your spirit of love
into every home and neighbourhood;
make us slow to criticise and quick to forgive.

Silence for prayer

All-knowing God,
teach us your ways.

Father, breathe your spirit of healing
into all those who are weakened or damaged,
whether physically, mentally, emotionally or spiritually;
give them the reassurance of your presence.

Silence for prayer

All-knowing God,
teach us your ways.

Father, breathe your spirit of peace
into those who are approaching death
and those who have recently died.
Help us to trust in your infinite mercy.

Silence for prayer

All-knowing God,
teach us your ways.

Father, breathe your spirit of thankfulness
into our hearts as we receive,
our minds as we notice,
and our lives as we journey.

Silence for prayer

Lord God, receive our prayers,
which we offer
in the name of Jesus Christ.
Amen.

Living life God's way

Father, in our Christian ministry to one another
we need more discernment and less defensiveness,
more stillness and less rush.

Silence for prayer

Father, teach us
to live life your way.

Father, in our national and international affairs
we need more listening and less bullying,
more giving and less taking,
more co-operation and less thirst for revenge.

Silence for prayer

Father, teach us
to live life your way.

Father, in our relationships
we need more understanding and less intolerance,
more encouragement and less condemnation.

Silence for prayer

Father, teach us
to live life your way.

Father, in our pain we need your comfort,
in our brokenness your forgiveness,
in our anguish the assurance of your love.

Silence for prayer

Father, teach us
to live life your way.

Father, at the hour of our death
we need your presence and your mercy.

Silence for prayer

Father, teach us
to live life your way.

Father, in you our every need is met and satisfied,
and we thank you for the personal love
you have for each one of us.

Silence for prayer

Father, you have given us life.
Help us to live it to the full
for the sake of Jesus Christ, our Lord,
in whose name we pray.
Amen.

Teach us your ways

Father, you know our motives as well as our actions;
bless our decision-making,
so that we do not make wrong choices in our lives.
Silence for prayer
Teach us your ways
and help us to live them.

Father, you know the strengths
and weaknesses of our Church;
we do not want to hide anything away,
but long for your advice and guidance.
Silence for prayer
Teach us your ways
and help us to live them.

Father, you know us,
and those we live and work with;
you understand the real reasons
for our quarrels and upsets;
we long for you to work your healing
in those hidden areas.
Silence for prayer
Teach us your ways
and help us to live them.

Father, you know the individual history
behind each person's revenge
and each country's difficulties;
we long for peace and tranquillity in our world.
Silence for prayer
Teach us your ways
and help us to live them.

Father, you watch with the sick and the dying;
you feel their pain and know their fear;
we long for them to know
your loving presence with them.
Silence for prayer
Teach us your ways
and help us to live them.

Father, your creation is indeed very good,
and we praise and thank you for all you provide.
Silence for prayer
Lead us, heavenly Father,
in the way of life,
as we follow Jesus Christ,
our Master and our Friend.
Amen.

PEOPLE OF GOD

We are your people

Our heavenly Father assures us that
wherever two or three meet in his name
he will be with them; in confidence, then,
let us bring him our needs and cares.

We pray that your love will spill out
through your Church to the world,
filling all teaching, all advice and counsel,
all authority and correction.

Silence for prayer

We are your people:
hear us, Lord, we pray.

May your spirit of forgiveness and justice
permeate the social and political fabric of our world,
till we are able to rule wisely, discuss differences calmly
and be prepared to negotiate rationally.

Silence for prayer

We are your people:
hear us, Lord, we pray.

May your light shine in our hearts
to show us our faults and enable us to admit them;
to shine through our lives
in the way we treat one another,
especially when we disagree or feel hurt.

Silence for prayer

We are your people:
hear us, Lord, we pray.

May your comfort and consolation
soothe those who are afraid or in great pain,
refresh those who are mentally or physically exhausted
and be a lifeline to those who are broken-hearted
or in despair.
Silence for prayer

We are your people:
hear us, Lord, we pray.

May those who have passed into eternity
be welcomed into your heavenly kingdom
to live with you for ever.
Silence for prayer

We are your people:
hear us, Lord, we pray.

We praise you, Lord,
for all the joy and gladness of our lives;
for the beauty of your world
and the affection of our loved ones.
Silence for prayer

We are your people:
hear us, Lord, we pray,
for the sake of Jesus Christ,
our elder Brother.
Amen.

All God's children

Father, we bring to you our longing for unity,
our desire for a closer walk with you,
and our concern for all our Christian
brothers and sisters.

Silence for prayer

God is full of compassion,
full of compassion and love.

Father, we bring to you our longing
for a world of peace and integrity;
a world of mutual respect
and international understanding.

Silence for prayer

God is full of compassion,
full of compassion and love.

Father, we bring to you our love and concern
for our families, friends and neighbours;
particularly those facing change or feeling isolated.

Silence for prayer

God is full of compassion,
full of compassion and love.

Father, we bring to you our desire for healing
and wholeness in those who are distressed,
uncomfortable or in great pain;
we bring our willingness to help
wherever you want to use us.

Silence for prayer

God is full of compassion,
full of compassion and love.

Father, we bring to you our loved ones who have died,
and those who are dying with no one near them.

Silence for prayer

God is full of compassion,
full of compassion and love.

Father, we bring to you our thanks for life
and all its blessings;
for the experiences we learn from and grow through.

Silence for prayer

Loving Father, hear our prayers
offered in the name of Jesus.
Amen.

The Church in the world

My brothers and sisters in Christ,
bound together in love and faith
let us pray for the Church and for the world.

O Lord our God, we trust in your promise to hear us
when we pray in faith.

Strengthen us in the certain knowledge
of your constant presence,
so that we witness to your love by the way
we speak and act each day.
Silence for prayer
Heavenly Father,
hear us as we pray.

Teach us and guide us to use the resources of the world
wisely and unselfishly,
sharing its riches and respecting its beauty.
Silence for prayer
Heavenly Father,
hear us as we pray.

Alert us to the needs of those around us
and increase our friendliness and understanding
in all our relationships.
Silence for prayer
Heavenly Father,
hear us as we pray.

Bring your health and wholeness
to those in physical pain and mental anguish,
and give your inner peace
to those overwhelmed with worries.

Silence for prayer

Heavenly Father,
hear us as we pray.

Into your hands, Father, we commend
those who have died,
for we know that in your care they are safe.

Silence for prayer

Heavenly Father,
hear us as we pray.

And now we want to thank you
for your constant love and kindness,
support and protection.

Silence for prayer

Heavenly Father,
hear us as we pray,
for the sake of your Son,
our Saviour, Jesus Christ.
Amen.

Children in God's family

My brothers and sisters in Christ,
as members of one family let us talk to God our Father
about our needs, cares and concerns.

We pray for the life, teaching and fellowship
of the Church, our Christian family;
help us to support and care for one another
as true family members,
regardless of physical, cultural
or intellectual differences.

Silence for prayer

God our Father,
hear your children's prayer.

We pray for friendship and good will
between all the different nations in our world;
teach us to enjoy the variety as richness,
rather than fearing it as a threat.

Silence for prayer

God our Father,
hear your children's prayer.

We ask for your blessing and guidance
in all the homes of this community;
as each problem and difficulty arises
may your loving wisdom steer us in the right direction.

Silence for prayer

God our Father,
hear your children's prayer.

We pray for all who have been damaged
by a disturbed or violent upbringing;
for children who are growing up
amid hatred and cruelty;
may they be healed by love.

Silence for prayer

God our Father,
hear your children's prayer.

We pray for those who have recently died
and commend them into your
everlasting care and protection.

Silence for prayer

God our Father,
hear your children's prayer.

We thank you for all the joys and blessings in our lives;
especially we thank you for the relationships
which enrich our lives so much.

Silence for prayer

God our Father,
**hear your children's prayer
for the sake of Jesus Christ,
our elder Brother.
Amen.**

Lord, comfort your people

Father, we remember
those whose faith is fresh and fragile,
those who labour faithfully in your service
through difficult times;
all who minister by word and sacrament
throughout the Church.

Silence for prayer

Come, Lord,
comfort your people.

Father, we remember the needs of the world
and the unbalanced spread of wealth;
we remember the leaders and advisers,
the peace makers and the law makers.

Silence for prayer

Come, Lord,
comfort your people.

Father, we remember our own relatives and friends,
our neighbours and those we meet week by week;
we remember the laughter and tears we have shared,
the hopes, dreams and fears.

Silence for prayer

Come, Lord,
comfort your people.

Father, we remember the weary and heavily burdened,
the anxious, and those who have lost their way;
all whose lives are filled with suffering;
all who do not yet know Jesus.

Silence for prayer

Come, Lord,
comfort your people.

Father, we remember those
who have come to the end of their earthly life
and those who have nursed and cared for them
and will miss their physical presence.

Silence for prayer

Come, Lord,
comfort your people.

Father, we remember your kindness and mercy
to us at every stage of our journey,
and offer you our thanks and praise.

Silence for prayer

Loving Father,
**accept these prayers
for the sake of Jesus Christ,
your Son, our Lord.
Amen.**

Father, live among us

Let us pray to God our Father
because he loves us so dearly.

We pray that the light of the world
may shine so brightly in our lives
that other people notice it
and are attracted to you
by the way we live and love.

Silence for prayer

Father, live among us:
live through our lives.

We pray that our world may stop
its noise, chatter and arguing
long enough to hear the angels
singing of hope and peace.

Silence for prayer

Father, live among us:
live through our lives.

Father, we pray for our families
and all our friends and neighbours;
may every relationship we have
be filled with your love.

Silence for prayer

Father, live among us:
live through our lives.

We pray for the homeless
and all refugees and exiles;
for children from broken homes,
and all who are destitute, malnourished or ill.

Silence for prayer

Father, live among us:
live through our lives.

We pray for all from whom we are separated now
through death;
may they live in your light for ever
and may their loved ones know your comfort.

Silence for prayer

Father, live among us:
live through our lives.

Father, we can never thank you enough
for coming to rescue us,
and we praise you now and in our lives.

Silence for prayer

God of life and love
**receive our prayers,
for the sake of Jesus Christ.
Amen.**

Teach us all to love

We belong to the body of Christ.
In his name let us pray to the Father
for the Church and for the world.

We commend to your care and protection
all who are abused, imprisoned or insulted
because of their faith.

Silence for prayer

Lord, by your example
teach us all to love.

We commend to your light and truth
all governments and committees,
every head of state, and all leaders.

Silence for prayer

Lord, by your example
teach us all to love.

We commend to your longsuffering patience
and compassion, ourselves,
with our frequent misuse of your blessings
and failure to serve.

Silence for prayer

Lord, by your example
teach us all to love.

We commend to your healing and wholeness
all who are ill or injured;
those undergoing surgery
and those nearing death.

Silence for prayer

Lord, by your example
teach us all to love.

We commend to your light and lasting peace
all those who have died, especially . . .
Silence for prayer

We thank you, Lord,
for all your guidance and loving care;
fulfil our needs in the way which is best for us
in the context of eternity.
Silence for prayer

Father, we ask these prayers
in the name of Jesus,
who shows us how to love.
Amen.

LOVING AND SERVING GOD

Willing servants

Bound together in the life of Christ
let us pour out our needs and concerns
before our Lord and Father,
who knows and loves us so well.

Father, we commend to your love
all ministers of your word and sacrament;
keep them true to their calling
so that their life and work
brings many into contact with you.

Silence for prayer

Lord, here we are:
use us for your glory.

Father, we commend to your wisdom
all who wield power;
help them to encourage
reconciliation rather than revenge,
friendship rather than aggression,
and flexibility rather than stubborn intransigence.

Silence for prayer

Lord, here we are:
use us for your glory.

Father, we commend to your peace and joy
our homes and all the homes in this community,
especially any where there is conflict or distress;
dwell with us, so that our homes speak
to every visitor of your love.

Silence for prayer

Lord, here we are:
use us for your glory.

Father, we commend to your healing
all who are in pain or danger;
all who are recovering from surgery;
all who depend on others for life and movement;
and who long for a friend who would visit them
and care about them.

Silence for prayer

Lord, here we are:
use us for your glory.

Father, we commend to your keeping
those who have left this life through the gate of death;
may they live with you in the light of heaven for ever.

Silence for prayer

We thank you for calling us
and we offer you the rest of our lives.

Silence for prayer

Father, we bring these prayers
in the name of Jesus.
Amen.

Use us, Lord

As members of the body of Christ
bound together in his love,
let us pray together now,
confident in God's promise to be amongst us.

We pray for all who form the Church
in its variety and richness throughout the world;
may the weak be encouraged and strengthened,
the wanderers return,
those besieged by doubt be given the assurance of faith,
and the jaded refreshed by your living Spirit.
Silence for prayer
Take us as we are
and use us, Lord.

We pray for all councils, committees
and governing bodies,
for those serving on juries,
for air, sea and mountain rescue teams;
that in working together in your strength
they may strive for what is good, just and honest,
so that your will is accomplished in them.
Silence for prayer
Take us as we are
and use us, Lord.

We pray for our families and our friends,
that we may be transformed and renewed
through the richness of your presence;
give us deeper insight, more awareness
and greater love for one another.

Silence for prayer

Take us as we are
and use us, Lord.

We pray for the poor and for the hungry,
for all frustrated by damaged or crippled bodies;
for those in prison, and those enslaved
by drugs, alcohol, hatred or fear.

Silence for prayer

Take us as we are
and use us, Lord.

We pray for those who have died
and those who are at present on that last journey;
may they have peace in the joy
of your presence for ever.

Silence for prayer

Take us as we are:
and use us, Lord.

Father, we thank you for all your glory
in the world you have made,
for all you have accomplished in our lives
and in the lives of the saints.

Silence for prayer

Father, we offer you
both our prayers and our lives,
in the name of Jesus Christ, our Lord.
Amen.

Fruitful for God

Chosen by God to be members of his body,
let us gather our cares and concerns
and bring them before our heavenly Father
who loves us and knows us personally.

We pray for the many individuals
comprising the body of Christ,
with all their varied ministries;
for those unsure of God's plan for them;
may your will be made clear to them
and may they be given courage to accept your call.
Silence for prayer

Lord, nourish us
that we may bear fruit.

We pray for the world and its areas of conflict,
political unrest, decadence and deceit;
that Christ, the Lord of all truth and life,
may lead humanity to desire justice, peace and integrity.
Silence for prayer

Lord, nourish us
that we may bear fruit.

We pray for a deeper trust in God among all of us here,
and the families we represent;
that we may spend our lives
in getting to know you better,
so we reflect your light more brightly
and can be of greater use to you in serving your world.

Silence for prayer
Lord, nourish us
that we may bear fruit.

We pray for the bereaved and all who mourn;
for those who have miscarried
or given birth to a stillborn baby;
for those who feel uncared for and unloved;
for those who must watch their children
die from lack of food.
Silence for prayer
Lord, nourish us
that we may bear fruit.

We pray for all the faithful who have died;
may they rest for ever in the peace and joy of heaven.
Silence for prayer

We offer you our thanks and praise
for the way you have guided us
and brought us to worship you now;
may we continue to praise you
in the way we live the rest of our lives.
Silence for prayer
Lord, hear our prayers,
which we ask in the name of Jesus,
our Saviour and our Friend.
Amen.

Pledged to God's service

Dear friends in Christ,
as we gather here in the presence of the living God,
let us ask for his help and guidance
in the Church and in the world.

We join in prayer with all other worshipping Christians;
give us an increasing love and affection
between individuals and groups
in every church and denomination;
increasing open-heartedness,
outreach and generosity of spirit.

Silence for prayer

Unchanging Lord,
we pledge ourselves to your service.

We pray for the breaking down of suspicion,
double standards and hypocrisy in our world;
that the nations may work together
to conquer the problems of food and water distribution,
so that our planet's resources are shared and not wasted.

Silence for prayer

Unchanging Lord,
we pledge ourselves to your service.

We pray for the homes and families represented here,
with all their particular joys and sorrows,
needs and resources;
that our lives may be practical witnesses to our faith.

Silence for prayer

Unchanging Lord,
we pledge ourselves to your service.

We pray for those involved in medical research,
and all who suffer from diseases
which are as yet incurable;
for any who are too weak or exhausted to pray;
for any who are desperate or suicidal.

Silence for prayer

Unchanging Lord,
we pledge ourselves to your service.

We pray that all who have died in faith
may rise to new life in glory.

Silence for prayer

Father, we thank you for your immense compassion,
understanding and encouragement throughout our lives.

Silence for prayer

Loving, heavenly Father,
we know you hear our prayers,
because we ask them in the name
of Jesus Christ, our Lord.
Amen.

We offer ourselves

My companions in Christ,
let us lay at the feet of our heavenly Father
all our cares and concerns for the Church
and for the world.

We pray for those Christians whom you are calling
to a particular ministry;
may they recognise your voice and respond to it in trust.
Silence for prayer

Lord, hear us:
we offer ourselves to your service.

We pray for all involved with government,
both in our own country and throughout the world;
may the way we govern
reflect the way we are governed by you,
our God of justice, mercy and compassion.
Silence for prayer

Lord, hear us:
we offer ourselves to your service.

We pray that we, and all others worshipping
in this community, may allow you access
into more of our life and personality;
so you can work through us
to spread healing and wholeness.
Silence for prayer

Lord, hear us:
we offer ourselves to your service.

We pray for those who have become locked
in their guilt, resentment, self-pity or hatred;
may they be released through thorough repentance
to the joy and freedom of your full forgiveness.

Silence for prayer

Lord, hear us:
we offer ourselves to your service.

We pray for all who have been brought home
to eternity, especially . . .
May they, through your mercy,
live for ever in your peace.

Silence for prayer

We offer you thanks and praise
for all this life's blessings which surround us each day;
may we grow in appreciation
and learn to perceive your glory more clearly.

Silence for prayer

Lord, we bring you
both our prayers and our lives,
in the name of Jesus, your Son.
Amen.

Walking where God is

Father, in love we stand alongside
all those who lead and minister in your Church.
We ask you to bless their lives and their work.
Silence for prayer
God our Father,
we want to walk with you.

Father, in love we stand alongside
our Queen and all the leaders of the nations.
We ask you to guide them in your ways.
Silence for prayer
God our Father,
we want to walk with you.

Father, in love we stand alongside
all whose lives are bound up with ours.
Work with tenderness in the relationships
we bring before you now.
Silence for prayer
God our Father,
we want to walk with you.

Father, in love we stand alongside
all whose bodies, minds or spirits are hurting.
We ask you to minister to them now.
Silence for prayer
God our Father,
we want to walk with you.

Father, in love we stand alongside
all who are close to death,
and we pray now for your mercy.
Silence for prayer
God our Father,
we want to walk with you.

Father, with love in our hearts
we want to thank you
for all you are and all you do in our lives.
Silence for prayer
Loving Father,
be our companion on the way,
through Jesus Christ, our Lord.
Amen.

Building on the love of God

There are places where the Church is weak
and complacent;
where we are deaf and blind to how you are leading us.
Open our hearts to hear and see you more clearly.
Silence for prayer
Father, let our lives
be strongly built on your love.

There are places where brutal force and corruption
seem to have the upper hand.
Quieten our lives and give space to all leaders
to hear your wisdom.
Silence for prayer
Father, let our lives
be strongly built on your love.

There are homes where arguments flare up
all the time, and people are sad and lonely.
Fill each home in this community with peace and love.
Silence for prayer
Father, let our lives
be strongly built on your love.

There are people with raging temperatures
and bodies full of pain.
Keep them safe and bring them to wholeness.
Silence for prayer
Father, let our lives
be strongly built on your love.

There are people from every country
who have recently died.
Welcome them into your kingdom
and comfort those who miss them.

Silence for prayer

Father, let our lives
be strongly built on your love.

The world you have given us to live in
is full of beauty.
We thank you for all that fills us with joy.

Silence for prayer

Father of Jesus,
accept our prayers,
which we ask in his name.
Amen.

Take all that we have and are

Father, take our faith and deepen it,
take our Church and renew it,
take our need and supply it.
Silence for prayer
My God and my All,
let your kingdom come.

Father, take our community and revitalise it,
take our government and guide it,
take our world and protect it.
Silence for prayer
My God and my All,
let your kingdom come.

Father, take the young and empower them,
take the old and refresh them,
take those who are damaged and restore them.
Silence for prayer
My God and my All,
let your kingdom come.

Father, take the suffering and comfort them,
take the frightened and reassure them,
take the lonely and befriend them.
Silence for prayer
My God and my All,
let your kingdom come.

Take the dying and whisper peace to them,
take the dead and welcome them,
take those who mourn and grieve with them.

Silence for prayer

My God and my All,
let your kingdom come.

Take our minds and think through them,
take our mouths and speak through them,
take our lives and live through them;
and accept these prayers
for the sake of Jesus Christ, your Son.
Amen.

PRAYER

Father, we ask you

Father, we ask you to strengthen
and purify your people;
teach us to be better listeners
to each other and to you.
Speak to our inmost being and show us your will.
Silence for prayer
When we call
we know you answer us.

Father, we ask you to unravel the tangled problems
of our world;
help us to follow you, step by step,
towards harmony and peace.
Silence for prayer
When we call
we know you answer us.

Father, we ask you to live in our homes
and in all hostels and orphanages.
Remind us to value the time we spend with our friends
and listen to one another with full attention.
Silence for prayer
When we call
we know you answer us.

Father, we ask that the sick and injured
will be aware of your comforting presence;
that the very old and the very young
may know they are safe and loved.
Silence for prayer

When we call
we know you answer us.

Father, we ask you to welcome into your kingdom
those who have recently travelled through death
from lifetimes all over the world.
Silence for prayer
When we call:
we know you answer us.

Father, we ask you to sharpen our awareness
of all that is beautiful, hopeful,
precious and eternal.
Silence for prayer
When we call
we know you answer us,
because we ask in the name
of Jesus, our Lord.
Amen.

Father, we want to pray

Father, we want to pray for all who work
to spread the good news of your love,
for all who face insults and danger in the process.

Silence for prayer

In all things, loving God,
let your will be done.

Father, we want to pray for our world's leaders,
for all in positions of authority and influence.

Silence for prayer

In all things, loving God,
let your will be done.

Father, we want to pray for the people we are fond of,
and those we find it difficult to get on with.

Silence for prayer

In all things, loving God,
let your will be done.

Father, we want to pray for those
who feel trapped by illness, oppression,
disability or guilt.

Silence for prayer

In all things, loving God,
let your will be done.

Father, we want to pray for your mercy
on those who have died
and on those approaching death.
Silence for prayer

In all things, loving God,
let your will be done.

Father, we want to offer you our thanks
for the way you love us and look after us
so patiently and courteously.
Silence for prayer

Father, use our prayers
to pour out your love into the world
through Jesus Christ, our Lord.
Amen.

God listens and answers

Father, we call to mind all who teach the Christian faith,
all those in training for ministry,
and those preparing for baptism and confirmation;
we ask for the Spirit to guide us into all truth.

Silence for prayer

Our God listens to his children:
our God answers prayer.

Father, we call to mind all those involved in education,
those who report world events and comment on them;
we ask for your wisdom and integrity,
your discernment and values.

Silence for prayer

Our God listens to his children:
our God answers prayer.

Father, we call to mind those who have influenced
our thinking this week,
those we influence by our words and behaviour;
we ask you to realign our priorities
and give us courage to live your way.

Silence for prayer

Our God listens to his children:
our God answers prayer.

Father, we call to mind all who are suffering
in hospitals, bedsits, huts and houses
throughout the world.
We ask you to restore each person to wholeness and joy.

Silence for prayer

Our God listens to his children:
our God answers prayer.

Father, we call to mind those who have
reached the end of their earthly life
and are meeting you face to face;
we ask for your mercy on them,
and on those who miss them.

Silence for prayer

Our God listens to his children:
our God answers prayer.

Father, we call to mind the many blessings in our lives,
and the ways you reveal yourself to us;
we ask you to deepen our understanding of you,
so that we can love you more and more.

Silence for prayer

Father, you hear our prayers.
Teach us to listen to you,
through Jesus Christ, our Lord.
Amen.

Longing for God

When following you brings danger, Lord,
or weariness or discomfort,
we long for your help.
Silence for prayer
In the shadow of your wings
we shall be in safety.

When we watch the violence and selfishness
of this world,
its bewilderment and fear,
we long for your peace.
Silence for prayer
In the shadow of your wings
we shall be in safety.

When we work through our relationships
and feel for those we love,
we long for your guidance.
Silence for prayer
In the shadow of your wings
we shall be in safety.

When our hearts touch those who suffer,
and know their pain and distress,
we long for your healing love.
Silence for prayer
In the shadow of your wings
we shall be in safety.

When those we love meet death
and we must let them go,
we long for your mercy and welcome.
Silence for prayer
In the shadow of your wings
we shall be in safety.

When we see the beauty and wonder
of your glorious creation and of your holiness,
we long for an eternity to praise you.
Silence for prayer
Lord, you have made us long for you.
Help us to find you in love and in prayer,
through Jesus Christ, your Son.
Amen.

Praying through the Spirit

Father, we pray through your Spirit
for those who do not know you;
for those who try to control you.
Silence for prayer
Great is our God
and great is his power.

Father, we pray through your Spirit
for a world which is bleeding and aching;
fighting and starving;
cruel and vulnerable.
Silence for prayer
Great is our God
and great is his power.

Father, we pray through your Spirit
for the hurting and hating;
for the damaged and the deluded;
for the ruthless and the wretched.
Silence for prayer
Great is our God
and great is his power.

Father, we pray through your Spirit
for those we love and cherish
and for those we have to work at loving.
Silence for prayer
Great is our God
and great is his power.

Father, through your Spirit
we thank you for the flow of your love
which fills our lives with colour and joy.

Silence for prayer

It is you, Lord, who prompt our prayers
by the inner working of your Holy Spirit;
so give us faith to wait for your response
through Jesus Christ, your Son.
Amen.

Trusting in God we pray

Trusting in your love we pray
for all arguments and conflicts in the Church;
for all who feel confused about their faith.

Silence for prayer

Father, you hold our lives
safe in your hands.

Trusting in your authority we pray
for all international discussions and negotiations;
for all who give orders to others.

Silence for prayer

Father, you hold our lives
safe in your hands.

Trusting in your gentleness we pray
for new-born children and their parents;
for all families in crisis.

Silence for prayer

Father, you hold our lives
safe in your hands.

Trusting in your wisdom we pray
for those who labour to find cures
and protection from disease;
for all who suffer in body, mind or spirit.

Silence for prayer

Father, you hold our lives
safe in your hands.

Trusting in your mercy we pray
for those who have reached physical death;
for those who miss them or feel guilty about them.

Silence for prayer

Father, you hold our lives
safe in your hands.

Trusting in your goodness we pray
with thankfulness for all we have received
and been enabled to share.

Silence for prayer

Father, we trust you
with our prayers and with our lives.
**Use them according to your will,
and for the sake of Jesus Christ, our Lord.
Amen.**

Father, we call to mind

Father, we call to mind the Church and its leaders,
all who minister in word and sacrament;
a Church divided, with problems, hopes
and responsibilities.

Silence for prayer

My God and my all:
my God and my all

Father, we call to mind the barren areas of our world
and the areas of abundance and wealth;
the crowded cities and isolated communities,
the squalid, the fashionable,
the oppressed and the endangered.

Silence for prayer

My God and my all:
my God and my all.

Father, we call to mind our parents
and all whom we love and care for;
all who cause us concern,
all who make us laugh
and all whose lives touch our own.

Silence for prayer

My God and my all:
my God and my all.

Father, we call to mind the malnourished
and the starving;
those living in inadequate housing
and those with nowhere to live.

Silence for prayer

My God and my all:
my God and my all.

Father, we call to mind the dying,
and those who have finished their earthly life;
those who die alone and those who grieve alone.

Silence for prayer

My God and my all:
my God and my all.

Father, we call to mind all that is good
and lovely in our lives;
all that builds us up, eases our loads
and strengthens our faith.

Silence for prayer

Father, we thank you
that you hear our prayers;
give us the faith
to discern your answers,
through Jesus Christ, our Lord.
Amen.

Not our wants but our needs

Where the Church is weakened by doubt or apathy,
by confused priorities, or lack of self discipline,
we commend it to the Father's love.

Silence for prayer

Father, we ask not for what we want
but for what you know we need.

Where the world is morally off course,
bogged down in ancient feuds,
and overwhelmed with disaster,
we commend it to the Father's love.

Silence for prayer

Father, we ask not for what we want
but for what you know we need.

Where homes are harassed and over-busy,
where children are frightened
or adults are coping in difficult circumstances,
we commend them to the Father's love.

Silence for prayer

Father, we ask not for what we want
but for what you know we need.

Where patients wait for and recover from operations,
where the helpless are learning dependence
and today's new babies are struggling into the world,
we commend them to the Father's love.

Silence for prayer

Father, we ask not for what we want
but for what you know we need.

Where the dying are entering eternity,
and the suffering bodies are at last
relieved of pain,
we commend them to the Father's love.

Silence for prayer

Father, we ask not for what we want
but for what you know we need.

Where experience has taught us more of your love;
where friends and neighbours have enriched our lives,
we offer, Father, our thanks and praise.

Silence for prayer

Loving Father, you alone
know what is truly for our good;
help us, then, to accept
your answers to our prayers,
through Jesus Christ, our Lord.
Amen.

Father, we entrust to you

Father, we entrust to you the small
and the complex problems
facing your Church throughout the world;
we think of all those in lay and ordained ministry,
and of each person worshipping somewhere today.

Silence for prayer

You are my refuge:
God in whom I trust.

Father, we entrust to you the local issues
where feelings run high;
the national and international matters of concern
and our longing for your kingdom to come on earth.

Silence for prayer

You are my refuge:
God in whom I trust.

Father, we entrust to you our loved ones;
those who are constantly on our minds;
those who frighten us;
and all who need us to listen to them better.

Silence for prayer

You are my refuge:
God in whom I trust.

Father, we entrust to you all who feel lost
or disillusioned;
those whose lives are plagued by resentment
or guilt;
all who suffer and need comforting.

Silence for prayer

You are my refuge:
God in whom I trust.

Father, we entrust to you those who have died
and those who will die today;
all who mourn and all who minister
to their needs.

Silence for prayer

You are my refuge:
God in whom I trust.

Father, we entrust to you ourselves
and the rest of our lives;
all our decisions,
hopes, sorrows and joys.

Silence for prayer

Father, we trust you with our prayers;
help us also to trust you with your answers,
through Jesus Christ, our Lord.
Amen.

God hears our needs

Father, the Church has its areas of weakness and pain;
we long to be truly and faithfully
the body of Christ.

Silence for prayer

Father, we thank you
for hearing our needs.

Father, the nations bicker and fight;
we long for a world where love
and peace prevail.

Silence for prayer

Father, we thank you
for hearing our needs.

Father, our homes and families have tensions
and misunderstandings;
we long for your wise parenting in every home.

Silence for prayer

Father, we thank you
for hearing our needs.

Father, many are sad, stressed, in pain or in need;
we long for your healing presence
to comfort and renew.

Silence for prayer

Father, we thank you
for hearing our needs.

Father, some die destitute and unnoticed;
some die violently,
and many grieve for their loved ones;
we long for your reassuring love and hope.

Silence for prayer

Father, we thank you
for hearing our needs.

Father, our lives are so rich with blessings;
we long to show our thanks in our lives.

Silence for prayer

Father, you know what is best for us;
help us to recognise it
and welcome it
when it comes,
through Jesus Christ, our Lord.
Amen.

We will not forget
what you have done

Father, in all the decisions and activities of the Church,
make us slow to rush ahead of you,
yet quick to follow where you lead.

Silence for prayer

We will not forget what you have done:
in you we put our trust.

Father, in all areas of conflict and injustice,
keep us clear sighted, and attentive to your will.

Silence for prayer

We will not forget what you have done:
in you we put our trust.

Father, with our friends, neighbours and loved ones,
with those we are tempted to despise,
give us opportunity to serve.

Silence for prayer

We will not forget what you have done:
in you we put our trust.

Father, on those who are ill and frail,
place healing hands;
in those who live fearfully, breathe peace.

Silence for prayer

We will not forget what you have done:
in you we put our trust.

Father, to the dead and dying bring rest;
to those who die unwanted and alone
give knowledge of their brothers' and sisters' concern.
Silence for prayer
We will not forget what you have done:
in you we put our trust.

Father, with joy we call to mind your love,
and marvel at your affection for us.
Silence for prayer
Loving, heavenly Father,
may we thank you for all that is past
and trust you with all that's to come,
through Jesus Christ, our Lord.
Amen.

THE JOURNEY OF FAITH

Travelling with God

Through the adventures of Christian witness
and the dangers, insults, mocking and anger
we may meet,
keep us, and all your Church, loyal and strong.
Silence for prayer
Come with us, Lord,
and we will go with you.

Through the local, national and international tensions,
through rows in the community
and distortions of the truth,
keep us and all people honest,
just and compassionate.
Silence for prayer
Come with us, Lord,
and we will go with you.

Through the interrupted nights,
the quarrels and celebrations,
the unspoken needs and wounds,
keep us and our children safe and loving.
Silence for prayer
Come with us, Lord,
and we will go with you.

Through the dark hours of pain,
the struggle with guilt and the damage of hatred,
keep us trustful and open.
Silence for prayer

Come with us, Lord,
and we will go with you.

Through the last journey of death
and the ache of separation,
keep us both in and out of time,
held firmly by your love.

Silence for prayer

Come with us, Lord,
and we will go with you.

Through the sunlight and shadows of each day,
through storms and stillness,
keep us thankful and rejoicing.

Silence for prayer

Lord, teach us not only to ask
but to trust and obey,
through Jesus Christ, our Lord.
Amen.

Faithfulness

Companions in Christ,
knowing the loyalty and faithfulness
of our Father in heaven, let us pray to him
for the Church and for our world.

Keep all Christians firm and steadfast in their faith,
with lives that witness clearly
to the power of your love.
Silence for prayer
Hear us, Father:
we come to do your will.

Guide our leaders, and all those in influential positions,
to uphold and promote Christian values.
all in charge of hospitals, schools, factories
and all community services.
Silence for prayer
Hear us, Father:
we come to do your will.

Be present in our homes and our relationships,
and increase our commitment to reconciliation,
encouragement and understanding of one another.
Silence for prayer
Hear us, Father:
we come to do your will.

Give reassurance and peace
to all who are anxious, depressed or confused;
and make us aware of the needs of others.
Silence for prayer

Hear us, Father:
we come to do your will.

Into your safe keeping
we commend all those who have died . . .
for with you there is eternal life, peace and joy.
Silence for prayer

We thank you for all the many blessings
we receive each day,
and in silence we pour out
our individual reasons for gratitude.
Silence for prayer

Father, in our prayers
may we not only ask for your aid
but listen for your word,
through Jesus Christ, our Lord.
Amen.

Courage in suffering

As children and heirs through adoption,
and knowing that Jesus shares in all our suffering and joy,
let us confide in our heavenly Father
who knows us so well.

Father, into your enlightenment and perception
we bring all whose faith is limited by fear or prejudice;
all whose living faith has been replaced
by the empty shell of habit.
Silence for prayer
Father, give us courage:
you are our only strength.

Father, into the depths of your wisdom
and understanding we bring those with responsibilities,
and all who have difficult decisions to make;
all those in charge of hospitals, schools,
industry and all community services.
Silence for prayer
Father, give us courage:
you are our only strength.

Into your tireless faithfulness we bring any
who rely on us for help, support or guidance;
any whom we are being asked to serve
or introduce to your love.
Silence for prayer
Father, give us courage:
you are our only strength.

Into the gentleness of your healing love
we bring all who are in pain;
all those recovering from surgery;
those involved in crippling accidents
or suffering from wasting diseases.

Silence for prayer

Father, give us courage:
you are our only strength.

Into your light and peace
we commend those who have died,
especially any dear to us
whom we name in the silence of our hearts.

Silence for prayer

Father, give us courage:
you are our only strength.

Father, we thank you for supporting us
and encouraging us when life is hard,
and for all the exuberant vitality
of the world you have created for us to live in.

Silence for prayer

Give us the faith to see that you are with us
in sorrow as well as in joy,
in darkness as well as light,
through Jesus Christ, our Lord.
Amen.

Watchful and alert

When the pressures of the day
fragment our peace,
keep us watchful and alert,
both for ourselves and for the world.
Silence for prayer
For who is God but the Lord:
who is our rock but our God?

When false values are paraded
among the true,
keep us watchful and alert,
both for ourselves and for our young.
Silence for prayer
For who is God but the Lord:
who is our rock but our God?

When our tight schedules
leave no time for being merely available,
keep us watchful and alert,
both for ourselves and for those who need a listener.
Silence for prayer
For who is God but the Lord:
who is our rock but our God?

When the injustice of the world
laughs at our insignificance,
keep us watchful and alert,
both for ourselves and for all who rely
on our solidarity with them.
Silence for prayer

For who is God but the Lord:
who is our rock but our God?

When we begin to take the wonder of
your creation for granted,
keep us watchful and alert,
both for ourselves and for every person
you cherish.

Silence for prayer

For who is God but the Lord:
who is our rock but our God?

Now let us spend time in silence
as we bring our personal requests
before God in prayer.

Silence for prayer

We thank you, Lord,
that you always watch over our needs.
Help us also to be alert to the needs of others,
for the sake of Jesus Christ.
Amen.

Lead us to yourself

We pray for all who spend their lives
leading others to you,
supporting and encouraging them on your journey;
give them your ideas, your love for others,
your joy and your humility.

Silence for prayer

Father, today and every day,
lead us to yourself.

We pray for our leaders and advisers in politics,
business, education and health;
for good values, integrity and compassion,
for courage to stand up for what is right.

Silence for prayer

Father, today and every day,
lead us to yourself.

We pray for our relationships with our neighbours,
colleagues and those in our family;
for the grace to forgive readily,
listen attentively and to be available
whenever you need us.

Silence for prayer

Father, today and every day,
lead us to yourself.

We pray for the frail and the wounded,
the harassed and the despairing;
for hope in suffering, comfort in distress,
and healing of body, mind and spirit.

Silence for prayer

Father, today and every day,
lead us to yourself.

We pray for those who have died,
and for those who mourn and miss their company;
we pray for the grace to die a good death
and live with you for ever in the joy of heaven.

Silence for prayer

Father, today and every day,
lead us to yourself.

We thank you for all those who have helped
and inspired us on our Christian journey;
for the experiences that have led us
to know and love you more.

Silence for prayer

Father, today and every day:
lead us to yourself,
through Jesus Christ,
our Saviour, Companion and Friend.
Amen.

INDEX

The World

The Nations
22, 24, 114, 126, 142

Poverty
56, 64, 128, 139, 166

Hunger
75, 85, 98, 131, 141, 142, 166

Refugees
58, 95, 131

General Needs
36, 40, 44, 114, 120, 122, 126, 128, 140, 142, 154, 160, 162,
166, 168, 170, 178

The National and the Local Community
Home and Family
15, 18, 20, 24, 28, 30, 32, 36, 41, 54, 58, 60, 64, 68, 72, 74,
78, 80, 82, 86, 95, 96, 107, 108, 110, 112, 122, 126, 128, 130,
136, 138, 142, 148, 154, 164, 166, 168, 172, 178, 180, 186

Parents
56, 164, 166, 168, 172

Children and Babies
94, 127, 130, 141, 164, 168, 178

Neighbours and Friends
10, 15, 20, 32, 34, 41, 48, 68, 70, 82, 100, 107, 110, 112, 122,
128, 130, 137, 138, 154, 169, 174, 186

General Relationships
10, 14, 18, 22, 36, 47, 52, 53, 54, 68, 78, 114, 116, 120, 127,
130, 146, 156, 160, 162, 174, 180, 186

Work and Industry
34, 52, 60, 84, 104, 182, 186

Law and Crime
41, 86, 94, 138, 139

The Media
50, 158

Education
158, 182, 186

Medicine
143, 164, 182, 186

Air/Sea/Mountain Rescue
138

People in Need
Sickness and Healing
10, 16, 18, 20, 22, 25, 29, 30, 32, 39, 41, 46, 48, 51, 58, 65,
66, 68, 70, 73, 74, 78, 89, 94, 97, 100, 105, 106, 108, 110,
112, 117, 121, 122, 125, 131, 132, 137, 143, 148, 154, 158,
160, 164, 168, 174, 178, 183, 186

Mental and Physical Disability
65, 73, 110, 112, 139, 164

Trouble and Depression
34, 38, 46, 48, 51, 55, 56, 61, 64, 68, 70, 72, 78, 81, 89, 93,
101, 109, 114, 121, 125, 127, 129, 143, 146, 150, 156, 160,
162, 170, 172, 178, 180, 186

Loneliness
21, 33, 94, 109, 123, 137, 150, 167, 173, 174

Fear

35, 36, 46, 48, 55, 66, 81, 117, 121, 126, 139, 146, 150, 160, 174

Violence and Its Victims

29, 36, 41, 45, 58, 75, 86, 96, 98, 127, 160, 173

The Homeless

48, 85, 95, 98, 131, 166

Addicts

45, 139

Suicide

45, 143

Caring and Carers

16, 59, 84, 88, 105, 129, 171, 182

The Dying and the Dead

12, 17, 19, 21, 23, 25, 29, 31, 33, 37, 41, 45, 47, 49, 51, 53, 55, 57, 59, 61, 65, 71, 73, 75, 79, 81, 83, 85, 87, 89, 93, 97, 99, 100, 105, 106, 113, 115, 121, 123, 125, 127, 129, 131, 132, 137, 139, 141, 143, 145, 147, 149, 150, 155, 157, 159, 161, 165, 167, 169, 171, 173, 174, 179, 181, 183, 187

The Bereaved

17, 21, 25, 31, 37, 49, 55, 57, 59, 79, 80, 83, 85, 87, 94, 99, 100, 106, 111, 129, 131, 141, 149, 150, 159, 161, 165, 167, 171, 173, 179, 187